Highly Effective Teaching Strategies

Highly Effective Teaching Strategies

WINNING IN THE CLASSROOM

● ● ●

Marc Hoberman

ISBN-13: 9780692790465
ISBN-10: 0692790462

Foreword

• • •

I HAVE BEEN TEACHING FOR over three decades and am amazed at how much I have learned from the children I teach. So many of them enable me to feel younger and even smarter. They have taught me the meaning of respect, loyalty and courage. When I was younger, I always said that if I were to win the lottery, I would become a teacher. I thought I would be a lawyer or a doctor; however, it has taken me over thirty years to realize that I did win the lottery after all.

That is why I decided to write this guidebook for new and experienced teachers alike. There should be no need to reinvent the wheel. It is my belief that the information enclosed can help you "hit the lottery" and become a highly effective teacher in a shorter amount of time. Many secondary schools have an eight period day. During that extra period of time I like to call the ninth period is when I believe the real magic takes place. It is my belief that a teacher's success begins and ends with the "ninth period." This is the time before or after school when a teacher plans, meets with students, contacts parents, and prepares for the day.

Most people want the quick fix, so I have made this manual compact, yet informative enough to assist you in organizing your life as a teacher. I wish you continued success on the journey to the greatest career in America. Trust me when I say, **ours** is the OLDEST PROFESSION!

Best wishes,
Marc Hoberman

Contact Marc Hoberman at info@gradesuccess.com
Visit us at www.marchoberman.com or www.gradesuccess.com

Marc Hoberman is available for presentations, consulting, and Staff Development.

You can also email Marc marc@marchoberman.com

Special thank you to Morose Leonard for his assistance in editing this book.

Table of Contents

CHAPTER 1

Planning

● ● ●

*"Our whole economy is based on planned obsolescence...we
make good products, we induce people to buy them, and then
the next year we deliberately introduce something that will
make these products old-fashioned, out of date, obsolete."*

Brooks Stevens

As far as I can see, much of education has become "flavor of the month"
oriented. This disturbs most of my colleagues because we find ourselves
teaching a different type of curriculum every few years. Besides, I don't
deal well with change unless I am the one initiating the change....but I
digress. Luckily, the one thing that does not have to change is our persona
in the classroom and the ways in which we impart information to our
students. This chapter is dedicated to the planning of lessons in a way that
can adapt to any content area. I have had the pleasure of teaching with "the
best in the business" and have included some practices of Master Teachers
in this book. Your professionalism need not ever become *obsolete*. As long
as you grow constantly as an educator, you will be initiating your own
changes and that is part of the formula for success in teaching.

Syd Farber, a close friend and incredible administrator, gave me the
best advice about classroom management. He told me that the **best** classroom management tool is a great lesson!

Walk the Walk and Talk the Talk

As in any profession, there are certain tools that you will need to look and feel like a pro. As Billy Crystal aka Fernando Lamas said on "Fernando's Hideaway" on *Saturday Night Live*, "It is better to look good than to feel good." When students see you in the classroom you want them to believe that "You look Mahvelous!." This applies to your teaching "wardrobe" as well as your clothing.

Attendance

This tool is very important. Students can't learn when they are not present. You are responsible for recording student absences and this serves many important purposes.

1. You need proof on paper, aka the computer, of how many times a student is late or absent especially during interim report and report card time.
2. Make no mistake: Teacher attendance reports have been subpoenaed in court. Students who use your class as an alibi can see their excuse vanish if you have proof that they were not present that day. This does not happen often, but if it does, you must be prepared.
3. When you can show a student in "black and white" how much he or she is out of class or late, you have a greater chance of impacting that child. Data is the new buzz word, so use attendance data to show students that you have to be in it to win it.
4. In most school districts, you can't fail a student for lack of attendance. However, you can fail students for work missed during their absences.
5. For students who are chronically late, try quizzes that start at the very beginning of the period and last only 5 minutes or so. Do not allow students who are late without a pass to take or make up that

quiz. Their lateness is disrespectful to you, disturbing to the class, and detrimental to their grades. **The very next instance when they come in on time, thank them and congratulate them. Let them know it is a sign of maturity that they arrived to class on time and improved upon their attention to punctuality. Positive reinforcement is the key.**

Some teachers disagree with me about thanking the students and congratulating them for things they should be doing, but don't you feel good when someone compliments you?

STUDENT GROUP CONFIGURATIONS

Varying the seating configuration in your classroom is very important. Unfortunately, some administrators and district leaders believe that a class should be organized in groups at all times. I am a huge proponent of leaving certain things up to the professional in the classroom. Pairing students in a Think/Pair Share configuration is very effective. Additionally, having groups of four or more to foster class discussion and "teams" of students who can work together, support one another and learn from each other. This is when true learning takes place.

RECORD KEEPING

This section discusses a necessary evil. I used to be a very bad record keeper. I am much better now, but still far from perfect. Luckily, I can teach organization better than I can keep myself organized. As my father used to say when I told him I would start smoking if he didn't stop, "Do as I say, not as I do."

Whether you are religious or not, your record book is your bible. Whether it be a computer entry or hand-written, it contains the students' names, grades, assignments, and more. You need to be organized and consistent in your approaches to record keeping whether you are using a computer program or entering information on paper. Below are some suggestions that should help you create an organized and effective record book. Make copies of your pages often in case the book is lost or stolen or in the all too common case of a lost internet connection or computer virus. If using a computer program, print updated information often so you can have the most current information at your disposal. For those who wish to also have information available on paper, the following strategies should be helpful.

1. Set up each page in alphabetical order. One page per class.
2. I like to skip a space or two between each letter. For example, If I have four students whose last names begin with the letter "S", I skip one line or more before I start the letter "T". The reason behind this is simple. Children leave and enter my class throughout the year for a variety of reasons, and I hate to cross out names every quarter or add new students to the bottom of the list. Another good idea is to write the names in pencil as changes may occur quite often.
3. I like to number my homework assignments and therefore list them in my record book by number and actual assignment and date. This way, if a student wishes to make up an assignment (yes, sometimes they actually want to make up missed work), I can look up the date or the assignment number rather quickly and help them organize themselves to make up work in a timely fashion.
4. I know teachers who have a separate notebook for each class with one page set aside for each student. They keep these anecdotals and record student performance, behavior, phone calls and have a PAPER TRAIL for each student. I did this one year when I worked in a middle school and it worked phenomenally well. It is a lot of work, however, but well worth the effort. Students are

shocked during a parent meeting when you point out something they did two months ago and mention the date and time of a particular infraction or issue. Hint: Try to record positive behaviors and experiences as well. **Positive reinforcement is the key.**

Lessons

It is now meat and potatoes time. You must have a good lesson plan that is organized and well thought out in order to present a good lesson to your students. However, I do **not** agree that this plan must conform to your school, district or chairperson's format. Unfortunately, especially for untenured teachers, you may be forced to adhere to a set format or template when creating your lesson plan.

My philosophy is that a lesson plan is only as good as the teacher. A great lesson plan on paper means absolutely nothing if the instructor is lethargic, not respected by the students, and ineffective. On the other hand, a master teacher can deliver magic each and every day regardless of how the plan is written. Below are the elements of a lesson plan format that I use in the classroom.

Learning Target:

Years ago, learning targets used to be known as the **AIM**. Where I currently teach, there is a specific format we are asked to follow, and I actually like it and feel it is beneficial to the students. Studies have shown that when students know what they are expected to learn on any given day, and are told how their knowledge of the material will be measured, they perform better. Explaining in detail what will be covered on any given day should begin with "unpacking" the learning target for the students. This includes using synonyms to assist them in understanding what they will be doing and responsible for learning.

Do Now:

This should be a review of the previous day's work, or something that the students can do for five minutes that directly relates to the present day's lesson. This is a great time for you to take attendance, collect homework, and answer any student's questions. (Sound like a lot? Welcome to teaching.)

Motivation:

I usually think of a question related to the lesson that will stir some sort of discussion in the room. You must have backup questions in case no one answers your initial question. Elicit responses instead of answering for the students. You want your lessons to be student-centered. Try to think of yourself as a facilitator in this regard.

Development:

This is the part where you actually teach the lesson. Hopefully there will be note taking and discussion. Of course, there will be questions but you must be sure to get through the lesson. I am sure you will have a set curriculum to get through by the end of the year so keep the kids and yourself on task. Fostering discussions through effective group work and teaming will be described in detail later on in this guidebook.

Summary:

This usually takes two minutes as you have students summarize what they have learned. I do not advocate lecturing to kids and therefore like to hear THEM do the summary. I know that I understood the material, but did they? Make sure and let them prove it to you. They are your critics and if they learned, then you earned yourself a four star review! This is often done in the form of an Exit Ticket. You can ask a question and have them hand the written answers to you on the way out. In my opinion, exit tickets can also be verbal. If children can't summarize effectively, you might want to try a medial summary in the middle of future lessons to check for understanding.

Following is an example of a lesson I have done while teaching Shakespeare's *Romeo and Juliet*:

Note: Our learning targets start with the statement...**I can** (the third word is from Webb's Depth of Knowledge (DOK) Wheel.) I usually try to use words that are considered level 3 or 4 from the Wheel. After the Webb knowledge word I insert the word **by**.

The DOK Wheel appears below. Notice how the word **analyze** is found in the Level 4 section. (Extended Thinking)

This is certainly not a full script of my lesson. There is a large amount of discussion and elicited responses that emphasize what I want to focus on for this particular day. I also take advantage of teachable moments and "go off script" if I feel it benefits the class to change the direction of the discussion.

MODEL LESSON PLAN:

Learning Target: I can **analyze** Romeo's love for Juliet **by** Shakespeare's language when Romeo first declares his love for Juliet.

My Learning Targets are usually shorter than the one listed above, but I wanted to include additional information for the purpose of explaining the lesson.

Notice how the students are told that they will be **analyzing** word usage and determining how the power of those words brings about an understanding of the love that Romeo and Juliet have for one another. They are already realizing what will be expected of them and what they should know by the end of the lesson.

Do Now: Write a brief journal entry describing what true "love" means to you.

This helps the students connect to the lesson on a personal level.

Motivation: What is the difference between love and infatuation?

There is usually discussion here and we come to a definition TOGETHER that infatuation is when you are so taken by someone that you do not see his or her faults, while love is accepting people for their faults and loving and accepting them anyway.

Development: *Romeo and Juliet* by William Shakespeare

a.   Petrarch-Italian poet who wrote about love. Petrarch was in love with love just as Romeo loves to be in love. I review the beginning of the play where we see that Romeo has just ended a relationship with a young girl, Rosaline, whom he loved, but she did not love him. After his experience with Rosaline and unrequited love he meets, and immediately falls in love with, Juliet. I review the definition of unrequited love from previous lessons with the students by eliciting the term and its definition from them directly.

b. I mention here that Italian sonnets, also knows as Petrarchan sonnets, dealt with love and because we see that Romeo is always passionate about someone he is often referred to as a **Petrarchan lover.**

c. We then read the next part of the play that shows how passionate Romeo is and how he is the essence of love and passion in a human being as he falls instantly in love with Juliet. Students then Think, Pair, Share the words that Romeo uses when he compares Juliet's beauty to a variety of things. We then delve more deeply into the meaning of the saying, "love at first sight".

d. After the reading I summarize by referring once again to the **Learning Target.**

e. I then assign and explain the homework and ask for questions. Always ask if the students understand the homework assignment. This way they can't tell you the next day that they couldn't do the homework because they didn't understand it. (Now that you have eliminated that excuse, you have to work on all of the others!) This is a good time to have the students write their Exit Tickets.

I had a student who couldn't do his homework because his grandmother died. After speaking with my colleagues, I found out that he was a most unlucky child because his grandmother died eight times in the month of April. How unfortunate!

Speaking of homework, don't give homework just for the sake of giving extra work. I was on an expert panel on a radio show in 2016, and when asked my opinion on homework assignments I had some very strong feelings about that subject.

Make homework meaningful or the students will see it as a waste of time. I usually read the responses out loud, (without disclosing names), so they know I read the work and students can then learn from their classmates. It is important to point out things that are missing in some of the homeworks as well as things that were covered in the exemplar papers. Students can learn from better papers, but they can also learn from work that is sub par. You should always discuss what could make the sub-par homework better, but allow the members of the class to make suggestions before you do. As time progresses, you should ask the students what is missing from a particular homework assignment. Peer editing, either in writing or verbally will assist students in being more adept at editing their own work. I am lucky enough to have a class set of Chromebooks and a Smartboard in my classroom. This enables me to show the work to the entire class at work. You can even take a picture of student work and email it to yourself, print, and then disseminate the work to the other students. I have found that when students hold something tangible, it appears more real to them.

TESTS AND QUIZZES

Tests and quizzes should be challenging and should check for understanding of the material that was taught. This is not your opportunity to trick the students, but rather to make sure they know the material and can apply it appropriately. In my first year of teaching, I had an entire class fail my test; I was proud that I was able to fool them. I soon realized that I did not fool them at all; they fooled me into thinking that I taught the information correctly. I tossed the papers in the garbage and told the students we both needed to do our jobs better. On the next test, I had an 80 percent passing rate. This was a low-level class and no small feat.

FOLLOWING THE CURRICULUM

More often than not, there is a standardized test lurking in the distance waiting to pounce on your students at a moment's notice. We are responsible for teaching our students information and strategies that will enable them to reach their full potential on a variety of exams in a myriad of disciplines. This is a necessary evil, and we need to realize that we do not teach in a vacuum.

You need to familiarize yourself with the curriculum. Feel free to ask as many questions as necessary. Ask your colleagues and your chairperson or assistant principal anything that you feel you need to know or have at your disposal to help your students succeed. As Mick Jagger sang, "You can't always get what you want," but try to get what you need. In other words, leave no stone unturned. After all, every finger will be pointed at you if your kids do not achieve. Keep a log of whom you asked and what the responses were so you have proof that you asked for assistance to help your students attain success.

DATA

Data has become a major buzzword in education today. My colleagues and I often use data to analyze our tests and determine if a large number of students answered certain types of questions incorrectly. I once noticed that a large percentage of my students answered inference questions incorrectly. This led to my creating more inference questions lessons and strategies that enabled students to perform better on inference questions.

Data can help you learn more about the strengths and weaknesses of your students. Data can also help you shape more powerful and effective lessons. I have become a proponent of using data in some instances but not all situations. At the end of the day, you are dealing with human beings, and there are some things that data is unable to answer. Read articles on using data in the classroom and make it part of what you do, NOT all of what you do.

Audio and Video in the Classroom

I love the use of audio and visual aids in the classroom. Technology has come so far that it is silly not to take advantage of how you can utilize it in your lessons. I use an application called remind101 to text reminders to my students. As mentioned above, I have had access to a SmartBoard and Google Chromebooks and Google Drive which has enhanced my effectiveness as a teacher immensely.

In your classrooms there are audio, visual, kinesthetic, tactile, and other learners and you need to address the many learning styles of these children as efficiently as possible. Differentiated instruction is not easy, but it is the only way to reach the many students with whom you come in contact.

Audio: I used to use cassette tapes and VCR tapes as well as CD's of song lyrics, speeches, and lines in plays to help bolster my lesson objectives. With the Internet and YouTube and a plethora of other technology at your disposal, your ability to impart information in a variety of ways is endless. This is not to be done instead of other teaching methods, but in addition to other strategies that you employ. Using a variety of strategies and technology will ensure that your lesson is understood by as many students as possible who benefit from a variety of learning modalities.

Video: I love to use video in the classroom but I am very much against the ever popular "plug 'n play" method employed by some teachers. I always supply students with a study guide that they have to follow and answer while the video is playing. I always stop the viewing at key points and have a brief discussion about the material covered. I also require students to write down at least one question about what they are viewing. This allows for active listening/viewing at all times.

INTERACTIVE TEACHING

Graphic Organizers
DVD
CD or Tape Player (Yes, some of us still use tape players)
Overhead Projector
Socratic Seminar
Proxima (hooked up to the computer)
Smart Board (You are really lucky if you have one of these)

The above items add so much to the teaching experience and help to motivate students. Most students do not need to be motivated. They are alive and energetic and always ready for action...**NOT!**

NOTE TAKING

If you teach something properly, students will remember it...plain and simple. Students do not take notes during their favorite song or movie but are still able to regurgitate everything down to the finest detail. Why is that? Because it was interesting! That being said, effective note taking is essential to student success since they are not as passionate about academic information as they are about the newest music video or song.

I don't believe that the average student even knows how to take notes effectively. Students certainly don't study from their notes correctly, so if you are big on notes, you need to monitor their work. It is absolutely necessary for students to take notes using a graphic organizer, abbreviations, and any way they can take down information for recall later on. Most importantly, note taking is a waste of time UNLESS they understand that they need to review those notes and even expand them later when they review. Studies have shown that learning does not take place until a student reviews material. Note taking is a skill and must be practiced constantly.

Proper ANNOTATION techniques must be taught and reviewed often so students learn how to engage the text **as** they are reading, not just **after** they have read.

1. I used to check notebooks as part of the quarter grade. BORING!!!
2. Brief **Notebook Quizzes** are a powerful way to find out quickly if your students are organizing their work properly. I ask four questions on a sheet of paper. The students have four minutes to answer all of the questions. If their notebooks are organized, they will have no trouble receiving a 100. If they are disorganized, they are up NOTEBOOK CREEK without a paddle. After all, just two incorrect answers will result in a failing grade of 50.
3. An example of questions might include the following:
   a. What was the Learning Target on October 10th?
   b. What was the name of the author we studied on October 12th?
   c. What was Homework Assignment #14?
   d. What is the definition of *personification* as written on October 18th?

If children were absent, they are still responsible for the work, so I do not excuse them from the quiz. This motivates them to get the work they missed since this is the easiest 100 they will ever earn. This works for Notebook Quizzes in all subjects. I use planbook.com so students can log on and utilize the student password key to access the work I am doing each day, whether they were present or not. Remind.com is a great site/app to have students interact with you as well.

I tell students to get the name and phone number of at least two students in the class so they can call them for work when they are absent. This was a given "back in the day" when I went to school, but children feel they should be exempt from any work if they were absent. Let them know that you missed **them**, and that **they** missed an assignment. Accountability is very important. With Google Docs, Planbook.com, school websites and other features, students **and** parents can have instant access to your lessons and students can see what was learned in class even if they were unable to attend on a specific day. If your school utilizes a student/parent portal, you can keep students and parents well-informed consistently.

SOCRATIC SEMINARS

I am absolutely in love with this method of teaching. It works for any discipline and any age level. It brings out the maturity in the students and it feels as if you are in a college setting. To help the students, use the A-Z sheet at the back of the guidebook for them to list characters and adjectives, nouns, etc. This is how I first introduce it to the students. They say the name of a character or mention something from the plot and then must expand the information. Others may assist them. Obviously this needs to be adjusted for other disciplines, and it can be a great review for upcoming tests and discussions. Below is a script of how I usually introduce the Socratic Seminar.

"Today we are going to learn about Socratic Seminars. Socrates was a philosopher who not only taught his students, but also learned from them. We are going to get in a circle and answer questions based on the material we are currently working on. You can pass if you wish, but you cannot pass twice. Once you answer the question, others will help you expand your answer."

I am the FACILITATOR of the seminar NOT the teacher. I have questions prepared and ask them to prepare one question on their own. We then go in order, clockwise.

The answers are amazing. The circle brings us together as a team and we have many beneficial discussions. A variation I created is to put one student in the middle and the other students ask him or her questions. You get one point for a correct response and one point for stumping a student. If you stump someone, you go in the middle but you must first provide the class with the answer to the question you posed. The person with the most points at the end of the period wins a prize. (A coupon for a slice of pizza, extra points, and other rewards work as well.)

A Quick note about Assemblies

Some people don't feel that this is part of your lesson, but I disagree. Before we leave for an assembly, I tell the students that they will walk in two lines in the hall, boys on one side and girls on the other side. These are high school students and they don't like this, but it really works.

Because of my humorous rapport with my students, I often threaten to make those who talk hold hands on the way to the assembly. They always laugh at this, so be sure they know you are kidding. Once, several years ago, the students were noisy and I told them they had to hold hands. I was more than shocked when I saw them holding hands upon entering the auditorium! I also take attendance before we leave for the assembly and once we are seated.

Always sit with your kids at the assembly. There are too many teachers who stand by the wall as if they don't want to be near their students. Some of the smartest people I have ever met in education are the students themselves. If you don't like them, they will know it immediately. You may want to sit next to the ones who usually have the most difficulty keeping quiet. They feel your presence and will be better behaved at the assembly. Make sure you sit behind your class. You can't see what they are doing if they are behind you.

You aren't the leader solely in the classroom; you are also in charge and responsible for your students at other times as well.

NOTES

CHAPTER 2

Classroom Management

● ● ●

*"It has always been my contention that no one has a corner on brains.
The greatest feats in business, as in virtually all of life, are performed by
very ordinary, normal men and women. Not geniuses. Peak experiences
of ordinary, normal people create leaders in business and elsewhere."*

HAROLD GENEEN, MANAGING.

TEACHING IS REWARDING, EXCITING, AND often fun. But make no mistake;
education is a business. We compete for salaries with other districts and
cities, federal funding is often based on attendance, and some districts have
been known to deny people tenure in order to hire new, less experienced
teachers. This hurts the kids, but keeps some taxpayers happy. Harold
Geneen is correct in saying that we all have the power to create leaders.
However, if you don't take ownership and maintain proper management of
your classroom, you will never get the chance to impart knowledge.

I have seen teachers who were absolutely brilliant in their content.
Unfortunately, they did not have the management skills to create a learning environment in their classrooms. This chapter can help all teachers,
novice and seasoned alike, create a learning environment rich in knowledge and respect.

MANAGING STUDENT BEHAVIOR

I remember when I first began my teaching career in the Bronx in New York. I was lucky enough to be part of a subschool where the toughest dean, Rose Clunie, resided. She was respected and feared by the students. She laughed when years later, I told her she scared me as well. When the kids misbehaved, a daily occurrence, I said I would send for her and they quieted down rather quickly. One day I threatened to call her on the classroom phone, and they continued their poor behavior and even began throwing spitballs at me. I soon found out what they already knew. She was absent! I never had control of my class; she did.

I immediately asked teachers with excellent class control if I could observe their techniques during my lunch period. I sat and learned from the Masters and over the years, I have honed my own skills to create, what I think, is a very powerful formula for managing student behavior.

It is important to note that although I think I have excellent classroom management skills, I still discuss strategies employed by other teachers and continue my own learning process.

It is not difficult to teach in a classroom where students are misbehaving. It is IMPOSSIBLE! The following is a step-by-step approach to managing student behavior.

First, all students should get a contract the first week of class. You have to decide on your rules; I can't do that for you. I often ask what rule number three is as part of my Notebook Quiz. You can ask any number on a Notebook Quiz (Always number your rules so you can direct them to the rule they broke quickly.) Some of my rules include:

1. No foul language.
2. No hats (Bad hair days are your problem, not mine.)
3. Raise your hand to ask or answer a question.
4. Never throw out your work.

5. Garbage gets thrown out at the end of the period (I hate when they get up and throw garbage away when I am teaching. It distracts me and is rude.)
6. You are responsible for all work even if you are absent.
7. The period is over when I say so, the bell means nothing to me. (I do not allow kids to pack up before I dismiss class. Those who do are made to leave last.)
8. Bring a Loose-leaf Notebook, two pens and two pencils EVERY day.

I don't lend pens, I rent supplies. They cost points or a phone call home. This is no longer the case for me due to an investment I made three years ago.

I spent $50 on custom made Bic pens. They have an imprint that states:

I was unprepared for class today. I borrowed this pen from Mr. Hoberman. I must return it after class. I used to never get back pens that I gave to students for the period. Now, 95% of the pens are returned. The message on the pens lets them know that they are borrowing my materials and it is a loan, not a "gift".

During class, I write down some of their rules and add them to mine, and the next day they are given the new contracts.

I have them sign the contract and the parent signs as well. I then make copies of the contract and keep one set and return the others to the students. Students have to keep the contract in their notebooks the entire year. I like to have an outline in front of me indicating the rules I would like to be in my contract. The first day of school, I allow the students to create some of the rules that will be part of the contract for several reasons:

A. Their rules are usually more stringent than mine.
B. They take class very seriously when they have taken part in the creation of the contract.
C. This allows them to have OWNERSHIP of some of the management of the classroom.

If someone breaks a rule, I never respond in a negative way. I am often sarcastic, and they find this humorous and always apologize. For example, if someone calls out an answer I say, "What part of **don't** call out are you having trouble with. Is it the word **"don't?"** Or I might say, "Feel free to call out." They know I am being facetious and quickly apologize.

If someone gets up to throw out the garbage I say to that person, "Do me a favor, remind me when we throw garbage away." They know this is a rhetorical question and keep the garbage until class is over. This way, I make it the student's decision to follow the rules, not mine. Sometimes I ask them to take out the contract and tell me which rule they broke.

Let students know that their signature means that they are agreeing to follow the rules as set forth by you. You are counting on them to be true to their word and honor their commitment. In fact, when they arrive late to class, I have them sign a late sheet that I keep on a clipboard. They will be signing many contracts in their lives, and this is the first of many. Although I want to set an example in my class, I sometimes throw garbage out during the period, and some students jokingly ask me to repeat the rule since I just broke one. When this happens, they are truly taking ownership of the rules.

While I agree that we need to be role models for our children, I don't believe **I** need to leave **my** cell phone at home. We are no longer children and we must teach them that with certain jobs and situations, certain privileges exist. We have gone to school, graduated, and followed all of the rules. Now it is their turn. I tell them they will be learning how changes are made, and they will have opportunities to change or adjust rules when they become teachers or leaders in other chosen professions. I also mention that well educated people have been changing rules for centuries, so they are in good company.

I have learned my greatest lessons and techniques from other teachers. In turn, I like to think that many teachers have learned from me as well. Below is a wonderful system for rewarding students that I learned from a master teacher many years ago and people have now learned it from me. It's always rewarding when you can pass the baton and share ideas.

THE CHECK SYSTEM

I am going to introduce this system in dialogue format. This is almost exactly how I introduce it to my students.

On top of the date on your papers you will write a check every time I tell you to take one. You get checks for correct answers, innovative questions, lending a pen or pencil to a classmate, giving a classmate the make-up assignments and for anything else positive and mature that you do. Checks are your key to success in my class. They boost your average. If you have a 63 average, you will fail my class; however, if you have a fair amount of checks, I will give you at least two more points so you can pass. A 77 is not a great average but a lot of checks will enable you to get an 80.

I will call for checks every two weeks. It is your responsibility to record checks properly. Some of you may wonder how I keep you from cheating and writing down more checks than you have. It's simple. I secretly memorize the checks of the same three people for two weeks. If your checks don't match mine, then the following occurs.

1. *You lose your checks for one month.*
2. *Your parent must come in and speak with me.*
3. *You and I meet with the dean, or chairperson or Assistant Principal.*

I take checks seriously and so should you. They earn you needed points and they cost me money. Every quarter the person with the most checks gets an Itunes gift card, 7-11 or Dunkin' Donuts gift card or coupon for a free slice of pizza.

I hand out a roster with student names where they write down the number of checks they have earned in a given time period.

(Teachers can vary the rewards as their money will allow. I often give rewards and certificates for most improved checks as well. Gift cards are also a great prize)

When someone does something that deserves a check I simply say, "Take a check." Sometimes I will offer many checks for one answer if the question is a more difficult one. Do not take checks away. Once they are earned, they stay earned. **Positive reinforcement is the key**.

After a few months, students are told to take checks automatically as they know they truly deserve them. When they are able to monitor themselves, a true partnership between the teacher and the student has developed.

I never really keep a totally accurate accounting of checks. If a poor student calls in 80 checks, and I know he or she rarely ever gets any, then I challenge that student. All students, elementary through high school love the check system. It is positive reinforcement at its best and they compete to earn checks. Be consistent and diligent in giving out and collecting checks. Be proactive and tell a student that he or she had a "C" average and now earned a "B" because of the checks. Remember, checks are only good for two weeks. Students have to start a brand new count every two weeks.

A variation of this method is to award coupons or fake money. Then the students can buy things such as a free homework, points on a test, and so on. I never use checks against a child. For example, I never say, "Take away 10 checks because you were bad today." Again, once students earn a check, it is theirs to keep.

This also fosters more class participation. I was a shy student as a child, so I am always cognizant of shy students I teach. Therefore, I give checks for a good homework, excellent behavior and other things in case shy students don't like to raise their hands often to answer or ask a question.

Remember: **Positive Reinforcement is the key**.

SEATING CHARTS

I let students sit where they want the first day; when I first meet them I ask if anyone needs to sit in the front due to vision problems. I always fill up the seats in front of me because I like to have a group of students near me when I teach, and I don't like them all over the room. I have used a Delaney book, and I highly recommend them. You can switch seats with a single card maneuver and you can keep attendance on the back of the cards. There are also educational apps that allow for seating charts that even have the ability to store student pictures. There is also a space for student data such as name, phone number, and address. There are some master teachers who have different philosophies about setting up where the students sit, and you will read about that in the chapter where I highlight these teachers.

Charts are also very helpful to substitutes. This is a good time to mention that you should leave a copy of your seating chart in a folder with a copy of your contract for your substitute. Leave an easy to follow lesson plan as well. Create these ahead of time in case of last minute emergency absences. Make sure your students know that your classroom rules are in effect whether you are there or not.

Various Seating and Teaching Arrangements

Cultural Respect

Students should not treat each other with disrespect in your presence, ever. If you hear a comment and ignore it, that is the same as you saying the comment yourself. Get angry and get serious...fast. I don't believe in the, "How would you like it if he called you that?" approach. Frankly, I don't care how the offending student likes it. I don't like it, and I do not tolerate it. I don't tell people that I don't see color in my classroom because I do. Everyone is not the same. We are all unique individuals. I work in a culturally diverse school and I have learned a tremendous amount about different religions and cultures and this is the most important lesson we can teach. Tolerance and respect is a must.

Writing Up Negative Behavior

When students misbehave in my classroom I always try to handle the problem myself. I call the student out of the room. I often get asked, "Why can't you talk to me here?" My answer is, "What I want to discuss with you is nobody else's business, and I am willing to give you my undivided attention so I would appreciate yours for a minute." **Never** get into an argument with a student in front of the class. You will always lose. You should never try to disable a "bomb" in public. If you have to prove that you are in charge, then you are **not** in charge. People who are in control of their room don't need to prove it; everybody knows. When I use the word *control*, my goal is for you to manage your classroom effectively, not control it.

When I write up a student's behavior I usually read it to the student and leave it on my desk. I tell students that if they can change their behavior for the rest of the period, I will tear up the form. However, there will be no other chance. Actions speak louder than words so if they say, "OK" I answer, I know you can behave, just show me that I am right. Ninety percent of the time I am able to tear up the written form. When a dean or administrator gets a complaint from me, it is taken very seriously. I don't send gum chewers and other inconsequential infractions to someone else. Handle your own problems and soon you will see that you don't have any.

For example, I do not allow students to put their heads down in my classroom. I never allow them to sleep. Some teachers do, believe it or not, but this is highly unprofessional. I take the student outside of the room and say, "If something at home is creating an atmosphere where you can't get enough rest at night, perhaps I can help you. That being said, you cannot sleep in my room. I am responsible for your education and sleeping is not part of that education, sorry. Let me know if I can help you with any problems that are making you so tired." Then I give the student a choice. He or she can sit up or choose to go to the nurse. Continuing the *nap* is not an option.

I put the onus to learn on the students themselves. I also let them know that I take their education seriously and will make them take it seriously as well. My statement that I am willing to help them diffuses any anger they may have. My saying, "sorry" gives the appearance that I wish they could rest in my room, but it is not a possibility since I take my job, and their education, most seriously. Then I thank them for no longer keeping their heads down. Just know that sometimes problems at home, health issues and other situations of which you are unaware could be making it difficult for students to stay awake.

Of course, serious infractions need to be handled seriously.

TIP: Go to the rooms where learning is always taking place. Learn from the Masters. Pick their brains. It's an incredible compliment to them and most are eager to help you. Borrow, Learn, and Pass It On!

NOTES

CHAPTER 3

Observations

● ● ●

"To observations which ourselves we make, we
grow more partial for th' observer's sake."

ALEXANDER POPE (1688–1744)

PRE-CONFERENCE

AN INFORMAL OBSERVATION MAY CONSIST of a pre-observation conference with your chairperson or content area liaison. You will discuss your lesson and the elements that you feel will make it effective. Typically, non-tenured teachers have six observations a year. Two each semester by the chairperson and one each semester by the principal. Tenured teacher observations vary from school to school. It's usually one a year but some schools allow colleagues to write some of the evaluations.

Often, the chairperson and/or principal might walk in unannounced. It would be silly for me to tell you not to worry. I would be right, but you wouldn't listen. I still get butterflies in my stomach and really want to be able to "strut my stuff".

1. Make eye contact with the students. Don't be too "touchy feely" with the kids but I sometimes give a pat on the back or shoulder for good work.

2. Use the *Arrow of Recitation.* This is when you take one response and "shoot" it to another student and ask students to add to or repeat what others have said. This way, the students are helping each other build answers. This is a mainstay of the Common Core and students learning from each other is the most powerful learning tool there is.

3. *Calling all students, calling all students…* Include as many students as possible. Observations usually include the number of student responses and how many different students responded.

4. Feel free to use humor. Don't use humor if you don't usually use it. It has to flow naturally, otherwise it can backfire.

5. Don't be a **different** teacher during an observation. Show the real you, not the Vegas version. You are a professional and a *dog and pony show* should not be necessary.

6. Dress appropriately, but this is my philosophy on a daily basis, not just on observation days.

7. If you know about the observation ahead of time, tell your students they MAY have a visitor who needs to check on their performance. Say nothing more.

8. Don't be embarrassed by inappropriate comments made by the students. Don't ignore them either. You can simply say, "That wasn't appropriate Steven." Then move on.

9. Make sure to give a typed version of your lesson plan to the person observing you.

10. At the Post Observation Conference, listen to all suggestions made. Do not be alarmed by negative feedback for two reasons:
    a. Your chairperson or administration is obligated to make suggestions.
    b. Some administrators just don't know how to give feedback properly or in the way we would like to receive it.

11. Always incorporate some of the suggestions in your next lesson your supervisor will be observing. Feel free to let him or her know that the previous suggestion helped you make the lesson even

better. You really can learn how to get better through the eyes of another.

12. Be prepared to tell the observer your thoughts on the lesson. You will often be asked how you think the lesson went and how you could have improved it even before you hear any comments from the person evaluating you.

I once knew a Master Teacher who was observed and gave an excellent lesson. She was told that next time her window shades had to be at least three inches above the windowsill. Some people grasp at straws and just don't know how to say, "good job." Many administrators are known to be very helpful during this process so just be patient and calm, and you will be fine.

I remember a time when a teacher had an appointment to be observed and the Assistant Principal had a last minute emergency and did not show up. Later in the hall, the TENURED teacher said, "I hope next time you tell me in advance when you are going to cancel. I wasted a perfectly good lesson on those kids!" I wish I were making this up.....but I am not.

NOTES

CHAPTER 4

Working with Parents

● ● ●

"Parents love their children more than children love their parents."

<small>MEDIEVAL PROPOSITION</small>

JUST BECAUSE KIDS SAY THEIR parents don't care does not make it true. I have yet to see a parent who does not care. I have seen frustrated parents, parents that were too young, and overworked parents, but uncaring parents...never.

I have not been at all satisfied with the number of parents that come to open school night. However, I recently learned that some cultures believe that schools are all knowing and that parents trust us implicitly to care for and educate their children while they are in school. Does your school welcome parents? Do you attend PTA meetings? Get involved in parent meetings in your school. Parents can be your greatest allies.

Be truthful when speaking with parents, but be professional. Log all phone calls and emails listing the date and time you called and list the name of the person with whom you spoke.

There are several ways to tell a parent bad news.

1. If a student is misbehaving, I always call the parent in the student's presence. I make the student dial the phone and ask for the parent. This way, the parent doesn't think that the child is injured and the school is calling for really bad news since the child speaks first.

2. Use what I call, "professional synonyms". Others call these euphemisms. Instead of saying, "Hi, Mrs. Jones, your son is a lying cheater. He copied off someone else's paper during a test. I can never trust him again."

   You could say, "Hello Mrs. Jones, I am sorry to have to bother you with this, but your son has left me no alternative. He copied answers from another student's test paper today. I feel that if he spent more time studying, he wouldn't have to rely on the answers of others. I would like to suggest that you talk to him about being better prepared for tests. If there is any way you think I could be of help please call me or drop me a note."

   I then tell the student that I am deeply disappointed that he cheated. I do not respect that, and I really expect more from him. If he does study and performs well on the next test, be sure to let the parent know. If you really want to throw parents for a loop, call them with good news. I am fairly certain that less than 5% of parent phone calls are positive. It might be time consuming, but it is invaluable.

Letters Home

Be very careful with what you put in writing. A good method is to have your chairperson countersign any notes home. This way they will be able to troubleshoot any problematic phrases. Also, if you get called in for a letter deemed inappropriate, you can prove that you went through the proper channels.

I like to use a checklist and a form letter. (Use school letterhead)
To the parent of_____
Please note that your son/daughter is having trouble in the following areas.

____ homework
____ classwork
____ behavior
____ etc…

Have your chairperson or AP sign the original and then you can make copies. You might want to make copies of letters you send home to keep for your records.

When you meet with parents, you may notice that they sometimes seem confrontational. They are often intimidated. They don't know how their child is performing and they may have had negative experiences in the past with previous teachers or school administrators.

1. Smile when you first meet with a parent(s). A good smile puts people at ease. (A fake smile makes people nauseous.)
2. Be as positive as you can and begin with the positive. Thank them for coming. Parents lose wages to visit the school. I know it is their child and their responsibility because they care, you have a great start. Then, if there is something negative to say, be professional, yet firm.
3. Don't just cry about all the bad things the student is doing. Don't mention a negative aspect about the student's performance unless you can offer a solution as to how you can all work together to help him or her improve. If possible, try to ask in advance if the student can join you.
4. I always say with the student present, "Have I said anything that isn't true?" I rarely have a student who disagrees because I have set the tone for improvement. I do not allow for a gripe session. We are there to explore solutions. Remember: **Positive reinforcement is the key**.

NOTES

CHAPTER 5

Administration

● ● ●

"Every country has the government it deserves."

JOSEPHE DE MAISTRE

BOSSES AND SUPERVISORS ARE PART of any business, and teaching is no exception. Administrators can be helpful and patient. Others can be impatient and a hindrance. Nevertheless, you need to manage their expectations as well as your own, and you will find yourself working for the administrator you deserve.

1. All administrators were once teachers. However, they tend to forget what it was like to be in your shoes. In their defense, they have to work with all teachers and some teachers are not professional and are often difficult to deal with. As much as I love having tenure, there are some educators who hide behind it and do not earn their salary. It is difficult for administrators to remove a tenured teacher who is inept and they are often frustrated by this fact as are parents and students alike.

2. I have been in an administrative position of sorts when I ran a Peer Mediation Program for the district and the pressure is enormous.

3. It is important to note that no one has the right to speak down to you and you deserve respect, even from your superiors. Not

all districts have unions to protect them, but think of "the rest of the world" where people do not have the protection of unions or tenure and still command and demand the respect they deserve.

4. If you are doing your job to the best of your ability, you will find that most administrators support you whenever possible. Understand though, that education is VERY political and people do what is best for them and whatever makes them look good in the eyes of THEIR superiors. Too often, expediency takes precedence over what is right and fair.

5. Make things easier for your supervisors. Help out when they need someone "in a pinch". Offer to help cover a class when a teacher leaves at the last minute due to an emergency. Help during assemblies. This is cooperation and fosters unity and camaraderie.

If you do your best job, then you will be seen as someone who can be counted on. Be pleasant, be professional, and give and command respect from all with whom you work.

NOTES

CHAPTER 6

Colleagues

● ● ●

*"If the finished parts are going to work together, they must
be developed by groups that share a common picture of what
each part must accomplish. Engineers in different disciplines
are forced to communicate; the challenge of management and
team-building is to make that communication happen."*

K. ERIC DREXLER

YOU NEED TO WORK TOGETHER as a faculty in order for the "finished product" (the students) to learn to work together and be successful.

THE GOOD, THE BAD, AND THE UGLY

If you thought some of the kids were nuts...You ain't seen nothing yet!!!

A school is not unlike a small city unto itself. Many faculty and staff members are very close and rely on each other for emotional survival. Some of your peers, however, will need to be medicated. Some love teaching because they love to gossip. There is a plethora of stories to be had in a school and there is no dearth of material.

The Good

There are so many good teachers who are also wonderful people who have taught me so much about education. Many people have counseled me and helped me avoid some serious situations have counseled me. To them, I am eternally grateful. This is not a career in which you can succeed alone. Take every bit of help you can get.

The Bad

Oh boy, this can get nasty. Suffice it to say that several teachers I know went into teaching for two reasons: July and August. They don't like kids and, trust me, kids do not like them. I don't know how they lasted. Our students will grow up to be the leaders of tomorrow. They will have horrible supervisors and bosses along the way and they will become successful in spite of these losers. Thank goodness for the bad teachers; they make it easier to pick out the good ones.

The Ugly

I have seen teachers degrade children.
I have seen teachers curse at students.
I have seen teachers hit students.
There are bad people in every profession. We can only hope that the powers that be will weed out the undesirables as quickly as possible. I can not tell you what to do when you witness a colleague act unprofessionally. You must do what your heart tells you….no more, no less. Do what you must in order to sleep peacefully at night.

NOTES

CHAPTER 7

Collaborative Teaching

● ● ●

"*THERE IS NO 'I' IN TEAM.*" Somebody said this, but I don't know who, sorry.

An entire book might not be able to cover Collaborative Teaching, but I do want to mention it for the following reasons:

a. I have done it for over five years
b. I believe in it wholeheartedly and feel it will be used more in the future

In the best case scenario, if you teach collaboratively, you will be able to choose your partner, but this is not always the case. I didn't really get to choose my co-teacher but the heavens smiled on me and I got an angel. We worked well together for years. She was a special education teacher, and we were one of the first teachers to use the collaborative model in our school district several years ago. I have also taught with English as a New Language (ENL) push-ins, and it is imperative for both teachers to learn to support each other for the sake of their students.

You need to respect each other and respect what each of you can bring to the teaching table. It is important to divide and conquer whenever possible. If you think that two people in the classroom reduces your workload, you are sadly mistaken.

You need to do lesson plans together and regularly discuss students in depth. This is a difficult job to do with someone else, but I think it is invaluable to the students. Just think of all the things that have to be delegated.

Attendance
Grades
Lesson planning
Parental contact
And more…

There are many collaborative teaching approaches.

1. One teaches, one roams
2. Both teach different parts of the lesson
3. One does the content and one focuses on various learning styles
4. Sometimes it is helpful for one of the teachers to make check marks while roaming next to the name of students to maintain a written record of how they are performing both individually and in a group setting.

Many times you have to learn your rhythm, "on the fly". You can not create this winning team overnight. My co-teacher and I weren't really comfortable until our third year together. We were always in the process of tweaking and refining our approaches.

The most difficult thing for me was to give up some of my territory. As I mentioned before, I tend to be territorial. Now, I am happy to let my co-teacher share the responsibility of delivering the lesson. It gives me time to visit with each student personally during the class period. I get to bond more with the students.

NOTES

CHAPTER 8

Emergency Situations

● ● ●

Great emergencies and crises show us how much greater
our vital resources are than we had supposed.

WILLIAM JAMES

YOU CAN'T SPEND YOUR ENTIRE teaching career planning for what might happen; however, you can be informed and prepared for certain situations.

FIGHTS

If you don't see a fight in your teaching career, then the school you are teaching in doesn't have any students. I have witnessed fights between faculty members, parents and security, teachers and students and, of course, students against students. I broke up a fight between a student and substitute teacher once and the student tossed a desk at the substitute and it landed on my foot. I broke my instep and spent five weeks at home eating Twinkies and watching General Hospital. At least I got to see Luke and Laura's wedding.

In the past, we were encouraged to break up fights. Now we are told that we are not covered (insured) if we get hurt while breaking up a fight since this is not part of our job description. We are supposed to secure the room and wait for security. You need to tell students that this is an emergency situation and in a firm voice usher them where you wish them to be.

The only time I jump in any more is if one of the disputants is getting brutally beaten. Please do not misunderstand: These type of fights are few and far between, but you need to know what you are going to do because the safety of others is in your hands.

Any drugs, weapons or sexual misconduct to which you are privy must be reported immediately. Be sure to document to whom you spoke and when. If someone is being abused at home and you do not report it, you and the school district can be sued! Remember, in most instances, you are a mandatory reporter. Always log everything. These "paper trails" can be very helpful to you.

In today's world, there are so many things that can go wrong, we need to focus on what can go right. We still need to be mindful of the Boy Scout motto, "Be Prepared". This can be applied to every aspect of teaching. You have chosen a career where the things that go on inside your classroom during a lesson are only a small percentage of what your job truly entails. The work is exhausting but extremely rewarding.

Our final chapters pertain to the most important aspects of teaching: Learning from the Masters, the students and YOU!

NOTES

CHAPTER 9

The Students

(The 2nd most important factor)

● ● ●

*"The children [on TV] are too well behaved and are reasonable
beyond their years. All the children pop in with exceptional
insights. On many of the shows the children's insights are apt to
be unexpectedly philosophical. The lesson seems to be, 'Listen to
little children carefully and you will learn great truths.'"*

G. WEINBERG.

THERE ARE NO WORDS TO describe the joy I have experienced from teaching children. Shaping the minds of our future is just a small part of the satisfaction I have received for over 33 years. Their thoughts and beliefs keep me young, and I have learned more from them than I can ever impart to others.

I began my teaching career in a school with 6th, 7th, and 8th graders. They overcame so many obstacles just to walk in the door each morning. I can't imagine that kind of courage. The day before I wrote this chapter I went into New York City with my wife and children to view the horrid destruction of what was once the Twin Towers. Even my sons were quiet and solemn as we viewed the debris. We then read through the many signs and remembrances that were posted. Later, I took my children to the Pokémon Center in Rockefeller Plaza. There, not one, but two former students I had taught fifteen years earlier approached me to thank me for being a good teacher.

They said they learned a lot from me and laughed often in my classroom. I introduced them to my family whom they had never met.

These girls were 28 years old and said that they were still trying to get good jobs and earn enough money to move into better neighborhoods. I truly believe that education is the cure to our nation's ills. I look forward to the day when we have all the money we need for education and have to hold bake sales to buy weapons for our armies.

Just four months ago, a student reached out to me on Facebook after reading my memoir Search and *Seizure: Overcoming Illness and Adversity.* He told me that I had a tremendous impact in his life, and that he was a success in business. I had lunch with him and his wife, and even though we had not seen each other for over 30 years, it was as if time stood still.

Although times have changed, in my early years teaching was not always economically rewarding. Even to this day my friends brag about their jobs and promotions which often include huge bonuses. Whenever they ask me what I make, my answer is always the same. I MAKE A DIFFERENCE!

You will come across hundreds and even thousands of students in your career. They are all unique. The quiet ones deserve your attention just as much as the seemingly more personable ones. If you just think about the wonderful teachers you still admire, I am sure you can understand what I mean. RAISE YOUR EXPECTATIONS. Demand the best that your kids have to offer. When your students know you expect 100%, they respect you because you are showing that you respect them and that you have given them 100% of you. **NOBODY RISES TO LOW EXPECTATIONS.....NOBODY!**

Take the time to get to know your students above and beyond what their grades tell you. They come from interesting families, they have incredible hobbies and stories that they can share with you. The best way to do this is to create a safe environment in your classroom. Some people mistake this "safety" as simply physical. Your students must feel **physically** AND **emotionally** safe with you. They need to feel that they are able to learn from their mistakes. Achieve this, and your rewards will never end and you will be responsible for helping to create productive members of society. Invest in our kids; your investment will outperform any mutual fund I have ever seen.

NOTES

CHAPTER 10

Learn from the Masters

● ● ●

Susan LoRusso is a personal friend and exceptional colleague. Her ability to captivate her students is unparalleled. Below are words of wisdom that she has been kind enough to allow me to include in this guidebook.

In 1997, when I was a novice English teacher at Chestnut Ridge Middle School, a student told me he and his peers could sense the competence of a teacher by the way s/he walked across the room and closed the door at the start of the class period. They could tell if you were going to be strict or a pushover just in that seemingly innocuous act. They could tell how confident you were in your abilities and how seriously you took your job, just by observing that small movement.

That observation has stayed with me for over twenty years. While I'm certain he was commenting specifically on classroom management, I think his observation holds true in other aspects of the classroom as well, namely expectation levels for students. If such strong signals were sent about management by an act totally unrelated to management, what other messages were being sent? What did my actions communicate to my students in regard to expectations?

Every teacher I know has a handout they give the first day of class where they lay out their homework policy, grading policy and expectations for the class. While informative to some extent, these "contracts" are NOT where kids get a clear message of your expectations. That comes in all of the nonverbal messages you send on a daily basis. How you run your classroom and what you expect from everyone, from your struggling students to your strongest students, comes through loud and clear every day in the things you do and say. Whether you teach an advanced placement class or a skills class for weaker students, there are things you can do to establish high expectations. Here are nine rules to live by to raise expectations in your classroom.

1. **Always say "Please", "Thank you", "God bless you" and "I appreciate it".** It's more than good manners. You are the model in the room. If you treat students with that level of respect they will do the same to you and each other. You create an atmosphere of comfort but also polite formality. We're not just hanging out here. We're here to do a job. I have my role and the students have theirs. Ask about the football game or grandma's surgery as the students pack up to leave. You want them to know you care about them, but there is a time and place for that. The class period time is for the business at hand. Period.

2. **Keep routines.** When class begins, there should be no questions as to what everyone should be doing. Work begins immediately. A "Do Now" to activate prior knowledge or something to read in preparation for the day's lesson will send the message daily that we are here to work. Likewise, nobody should pack up and get ready to leave before the bell rings. Work until the bell. This isn't just for classroom management but also to send the message that time will not be wasted. If you take the work you do seriously, they will as well.

3. **If a homework assignment is due, collect it first thing in the class period.** You send a message that it is important and a priority for you, therefore it should be for them as well. Walk around yourself and collect it from each student. Make eye contact so they know you know they are handing it in, or not. Make a comment about the title or opening for immediate feedback. If a student doesn't have it, urge him or her to get it in tomorrow so some type of credit can be earned. Do not ask why they don't have it. You'll

get a hundred excuses and reasons why they don't have it; some legitimate and some fabricated. It doesn't matter why the homework isn't here. If you get into what's a "good" reason and what's not a "good enough" reason you're focusing on the wrong thing. Then it can be perceived you're giving some kids sympathy and not others. Then you lose credibility. When a student hands the assignment in the next day, make a point to give students kudos for righting their ship.

4. **Homework assignments should be returned to students as quickly as possible**. You ask them to take it seriously, you should show you do as well. It's easy to get bogged down in paperwork, but I've found giving fewer, more meaningful assignments helps raise the bar and give me time to return work without more assignments piling in on an endless assembly line..

5. **Always grade and comment on everything you assign**. Even if you use a holistic approach, there should be some acknowledgement of the students' progress on their work. A student will not give their best effort if they know you are just putting a check on the top of the page and not even reading it. If students see you are putting effort into grading, they will be more likely to put their best effort into doing the work.

6. **Comment on what they do well and what they need to work on**. There isn't an exact ratio of compliments to criticisms; once you know your students and their abilities you can individualize their comments. A struggling writer may need more positive comments than negative at least in the beginning of the year. You want them encouraged and feeling good about what they are doing well so they will be more likely to push themselves in other areas. Don't lie or sugar coat things, but there are always a few things even the weakest writer does well. On the other side of the coin, don't point out every single mistake. Focus on the most pressing 1 or 2 things they need to fix. What's your goal? To improve their writing. You can only do that if they are willing to write. If they shut down, you

can't make them better. Conversely, even your strongest writers can always improve on something. Writing is never "perfect"; it is an ever evolving process.

7. **Always show an exemplar and review a few general areas of strength and weakness.** Whether you show the model before or after depends on the strength of the writers. Show it first to weaker writers to give them something to aspire to and show it afterwards to strong writers so they can see the little things that make one piece "better" than another. Either way, an exemplar helps the student see their work as it compares to the level of expectation. What constitutes an exemplar can be up to you. Maybe you have a piece that is less than perfect for weak writers to see a piece can have flaws and still be considered "good". Maybe you want a piece that is just a little beyond the writers in the room to be an aspirational piece that drives the strong writers to do better. You'll need to "read the room" and then decide what message you want to send by showing the piece. Obviously, using a piece written by a student in the class is the most beneficial..

8. **Modulate the specifics of your expectations without lowering expectations.** If you're working with struggling writers, their goals should be individualized and attainable, but also a stretch. If they struggle with paragraphing, perhaps a full essay is better put on the backburner initially. Have them build stamina and then assign the essay. Some may still struggle, but if they've written five or six good paragraphs, it will be easier for them to see stringing them together for an essay is not too daunting. The students should never be given a pass on a harder type of assignment because s/he struggles. It may take twice as long and require levels upon levels of scaffolding, but that struggling writer has to complete the assignment; it's very likely they will be required to take the same state assessment as the strong writer. Don't ever assume the student can't. Can't is not an option. You may need to "hold their hand" a bit longer, but they can get there.

9. **Treat strong writers as struggling writers**. As teachers, it's easy to see a well written assignment, especially after seeing many written poorly, and just give it a perfect score and move on. Everything is relative and it is easy to just say the student "got it" and spend our time and energy on the struggling writer. Look at this high school writing in the context of college writing and it is likely a different story. Looking at my own writing from college, and even getting writing samples from friends of mine who teach college, help set expectations for strong writers. Don't let them off the hook. Maybe they have the content down pat, but their diction or syntax could use work. Many strong writers I've encountered play it very safe. They are skilled enough to do what the assignment asks and never push themselves further than that. What if content was only 50% of how they are to be graded? What if their word choice, structure and sentenced development weighed just as much? Push strong writers to try new things and develop their style. As they move on to college and beyond, the way you say something is just as, if not more important, than what you say.

Lastly, think about the messages you are sending on a daily basis, verbal and nonverbal, formal and informal. Be sure you are consistent and patient in your treatment of each student. Push them to be their best in their work and behavior. Reward their accomplishments and encourage their development. You are constantly communicating your expectations...even when you don't think you are.

Michele Bond is a close friend and incredible educator. The "bond" she creates with her students is second to none, and her commitment to high expectations is legendary. The daughter of two "old-school" teachers, Michele has touched the lives of countless youngsters who stay in contact with her years after they have graced the halls of public school. Because I am always curious about the ways she creates success in her classes, I decided to include her approach to teaching in a question and answer format.

1. What does your first day of class look and sound like? What do you say to your new students?

I try to make my first day of class a bit different from the other classes. I spend a few minutes telling the students what they need for class and I distribute a contract for the students and parents to sign. I allow the students to sit where they want and ask them to keep those seats for the next couple of days so that I can learn their names as quickly as possible. Within 2-3 days I know all of their names and I know they respect and appreciate that. The majority of the period is spent doing a "get to know you exercise". Depending on the course we will discuss different topics. For my seniors, we spend time talking about the last year of high school, the college application process and why public speaking, (I teach Speech Class), is the greatest fear among people. With my sophomore English students, we discuss what's different about sophomore year, welcoming challenges and getting involved in school programs and extracurricular activities. I do not spend the period talking about "the rules". This conversation lasts less than 3 minutes. The students learn that all school rules are my rules....... They come to learn that the main rule of the room is to respect everyone in it. My room runs on the common sense principle-don't talk when someone else is talking, lateness isn't tolerated, and if it doesn't seem like the right thing to do, it probably isn't. I am a very straight forward person-I do not sugarcoat.

2. What is your communications strategy with students and parents?

I like to be in touch with parents, I feel it's crucial to the student's success. Parents and students have my email address and I post all grades on the school portal. A student's grade should never be a surprise to anyone. I don't wait for mid quarter progress reports and report cards to alert parents of grades. Progress reports are sent home and signed at least one other time per quarter. Of course a parent is contacted as soon as a drastic change in behavior and/or grades is displayed.

3. How do you deal with inappropriate behavior?
In all honesty, I have very few behavioral issues. I handle all situations on my own. I always start with a private conversation with the student. It usually doesn't have to go any further than that. Occasionally, I have to contact a parent......but that is usually for lateness, not inappropriate behavior.

4. What are your expectations of administrators, guidance counselors, and other staff in the school?
My expectation is for everyone to do his/her job to the best of his/her ability. Professionalism and consistency are what matters most to me. Our students need structure and need to see that situations are handled fairly and for the benefit of the school.

5. How do you deal with students who don't do homework? (Either once in a while, often, or never)
Every year there are a handful of students who refuse to do homework. For my seniors and honors students, homework is not accepted late. (Of course everyone deserves a mulligan and extenuating circumstances arise). My Regents level students are allowed to turn in homework one day late, but with a penalty. Honestly, they have grown accustomed to turning work in late previously, and it takes them a while to adjust to my policy. Furthermore, I GRADE EVERYTHING........so the students learn quickly what a zero really means. I do not believe in just "checking" an assignment that is turned in. The students need to feel validated ....and I want them to know that I wouldn't assign it if it weren't important.

6. What is your policy on offering extra help? Do students have to put forth an effort in class before you give them your personal time?
Extra help is available any day by appointment. I am very flexible. If we have a common free period we can meet then. If not, they can come into

school early (many work or play a sport after school) or we can meet after school. I will never deny a student extra help. However, if there is a student who has been apathetic throughout class time, who then asks for extra help, I will have that conversation with them when they attend extra help. Once a student attends extra help, they rarely disappoint in class.

7. Why do you feel that students who have you as a teacher often work harder and more seriously than they do in other classrooms?
That's a tough question to answer. Maybe you should ask the students! All I can say is that I practice what I preach. I think that they see how hard I work and how much I want them to succeed. Although I have very high expectations, my students know it comes from a good place… .I wouldn't have high expectations if I didn't think students could meet them. I genuinely care about them and that's seen in my involvement in their extracurricular activities, attendance at games, shows, and induction ceremonies. I also tell them that by the end of the school year I would love to be able to write them a glowing letter of recommendation for college. They know I won't write one if I don't believe in what I am writing.

8. Since you are a tennis coach, is there a crossover between your coaching philosophy and your teaching philosophy?
I carry a similar philosophy in all facets of my life…..I tell my students that my personal mantra is to remember that "My name is attached to everything I do." ……It's about having pride in everything and to always be the best version of yourself. So, if you choose to do something, no matter what it is (work, job, sports etc) do it to the best of your ability. I also tell them that "common sense should dictate your actions."

9. How do you deal with plagiarism?
I spend some time at the start of the school year explaining what plagiarism is…….and that there is a difference between direct and indirect

plagiarism. I teach paraphrasing, quoting and citing ....and spend a lot of time on those skills. Unfortunately, our school does not have a clear cut policy for plagiarism. I think it's crucial that we have one with penalties of varying degrees. In my class, those who commit blatant plagiarism such as cutting and pasting from a site, or copying from another student, receive a zero and I do call their parents. Furthermore, I keep those papers on file. Those that have plagiarized parts or random lines meet with me and we discuss the areas in question and they are asked to rewrite the paper with a penalty.

10. There is a strong bond between you and many of your students. If you had to delve deep, what do you think is the reason for the strong relationships that you have with past and present students?

In a nutshell, I love my job and the students know it. I can't think of a job that could be more rewarding. I like to believe that I am teaching much more than the subject of English. Yes, my students leave my room with stronger reading, writing and thinking skills, but they also leave with much more! The role of a teacher is just one hat I wear. Many of my students see me as a coach, mentor, friend, guidance counselor, and/or school parent. When they come back to visit during and after their college years, it's not the stories we read, or the essays we've written, that they say they remember most.........Rather it's the confidence they gained, the life skills they acquired, and the relationship we built that they treasure most. They know that they can count on me long after their year(s) in my classroom are over.

The final MASTER is **Chris Ferraro**. More than a decade ago my wife and I were thinking about having my older son leave his zoned high school and become a student in the high school where I taught. Although we never made the change, I told my principal that if my son were to attend classes at my school, Chris Ferraro would have to be one of his teachers. Enough said.

In My Classroom
By Christopher Ferraro

> *"...thank you for treating us like adults...tell it to us like it is...*
> *thank you for teaching your class like it meant something..."*

> – FORMER STUDENT, CLASS OF 2005

Several years ago, as we approached the holidays, I received a card from a student I had not seen in many years. It was late December, and I was staring down the twin barrels of upcoming midterms with struggling students and a rapidly approaching holiday for which I had not quite prepared. The weather was turning cold and I was getting tired. The next two minutes I spent reading this card undid much of the anguish I had been feeling. This former student, whom I had only taught for two years before her family moved away, had written the most eloquent thank you I have ever seen. The aforementioned quotes do not do it justice. For me, it was a *Hallmark* moment but it also left me stunned.

After rereading the card, I shared the quotes above with a colleague and told her I was amazed that this student thanked me for teaching my class as if it were important. "Didn't everyone do the same thing?" I asked. My colleague smiled and politely told me that was not the case. This led me to an evaluation of how I teach. Was what I was doing so different from the things others were doing? Did anyone really get in front of the class and inform the students that the topic of the day was not really important or something they would never use but that the state required they teach it? If so, what the heck were they thinking?

Having been asked to analyze what I do and how I do it brought me right back to this student's card. Without realizing it at the time, I feel that she encapsulated who I am as a teacher and why I am successful (usually) at what I do. I have broken it down into the following constituent parts.

1. *My class is CRITICALLY important and so is yours regardless of what you teach.* I teach Global History on the ESL, Regents, Honors and

Advanced Placement levels and what drives me with each of these groups is the knowledge that my class may be one of the last times students will ever be exposed to this material. If they are going to be a functional part of the civilized world, be able to understand the news, vote, and understand the forces at work that are reshaping society, then I damn well better do a good job. For my ESL and Regents kids who may be off to a trade school or an apprenticeship after my class, it is doubly important that they understand how historical events shaped the current world. This will be their last class in Global History! My honors and AP students have different issues. Taking any History class on the university level will require critical thinking skills as well as strong background knowledge that I must impart to them. In some cases, they may obtain college credit because of my class and this means they really need to have a good understanding of historical trends because when they get to their next university class, it will be expected that they already have prior knowledge and a frame of reference. Just a cursory glance at issues in the world today, ISIS, Al-Qaeda, Crimea and Eastern Europe and North Korea (just to name a very few hot spots) and one realizes how important it is that I put my students in a place where they can begin to understand what is going on around them. Certainly some topics are more important and interesting to teach than others but one needs to remember that minutiae are not as important as understanding big concepts such as dictatorships or the role of religions in the modern world.

2. *I am the expert in my room.* Years ago I overheard a teacher say that she disliked the Honors class because they asked too many questions (that she couldn't answer), always demanded an explanation and had parents who called the school too often for her liking. This teacher often told the students that their question was good when she couldn't answer them and that they should look it up for extra credit. This is another method extolled in education programs by college professors who haven't taught high school. The students see it as a sign of weakness... because it is. I'm not saying you should

know everything but you should be able to given the student some kind of answer to most questions. I don't know Stalin's shoe size (student question) and would wonder about anyone who did, but I can answer most questions about his motivations and actions. When I was a student teacher, someone gave me the advice to "stay one chapter ahead of the kids in the text." I laughed at this then as I asked myself if it were really possible that someone didn't know their history well enough to be able to answer student questions. After three years of majoring in modern European History I was ready to teach wasn't I? Then I got my first job and was handed Global History I, essentially, ancient history. At my college there were zero ancient history courses and even if there had been, I probably wouldn't have taken it. I was ready to lose my mind. So I went to the bookstore and started buying history books on my new course. Twenty years later I am still learning.

I had to be the expert in my room and I made it happen. Yes, it was work and it was totally worth it. Later that year I began my first Master's degree and I had a choice. I could take courses in European history with which I was familiar, or I could branch out. I took Chinese, Japanese and Mongolian history courses with a world renowned historian, Dr. Morris Rossabi at Queens College, and this played a critical role in my career in the years to come. Just two years later, I was asked to teach Advanced Placement World History with those very same students about whom my colleague had complained. Again, I was nervous despite my newly acquired knowledge of Asian history. So, I took a one-week College Board course on World History, bought every book that was recommended to me and made sure that I could answer every question being asked. This did not happen overnight. To this day, I purchase 3-4 world history books every summer and continue to build my knowledge. I joined the World History Association and read their journal. Yes, there is work outside of the classroom. This is what professionals do. In the classroom, this translates into a better understanding of my course and an ability to make connections and see the course very differently that I once did. My regents and ESL students will simply tell you that I am funny because I can make jokes about the intimate details of history. This is their way of saying I know my stuff.

3. *Classroom materials make all the difference.* When I was a rookie teacher I was assigned to a public high school in Astoria, Queens. I loved it. The kids were interested, asked questions and we debated a lot. My materials were wanting, but I asked good questions and could really engage a class. When I got to my current school, I realized (slowly) that the makeup of the kids was different and that debate and discussion wasn't going to work as I had planned. The race was on to find materials that the students would find engaging. Presently, I have a library of political cartoons, propaganda art, charts, graphs, quotes and pictures that form the basis for all my lessons. These students are visual and I play directly to that strength. My very first class with sophomores, I show a slide of a criminal in medieval France who is chained to four horses that are slowly pulling him apart as the crowd cheers. A good teacher can come up with about fifteen questions from such a document and get the students to draw several conclusions. It never fails. Teaching this is the easy part. Finding the documents to make it happen is the work.

4. *Classroom control and student discipline are skills to be mastered.* The first three topics in this essay will go a long ways towards a controlled classroom. If you care about your topic and are really interested in teaching it and find good materials, you are halfway there. The other half, however, is where many struggle. As of this writing, I have been teaching in my school for eighteen years. I have a no nonsense reputation that has been crafted over time. Students run to get to my class on time. Sadly, the incoming freshman have no knowledge of this, and I will have several sections of freshman classes this year. I can tell you exactly how this will go. Some

teachers tell me that they allow students to sit wherever they want. Many college education professors think this is great. You only move the students if they misbehave. I am from a different school. I feel letting the students sit wherever they want (next to their friends) allows them to get too comfortable too quickly. Students in my class are seated alphabetically with allowances for vision problems and the like. The message is sent one minute into the first class. I am in charge. Some teachers don't do this and they are successful, but this method works best for me. Seating the students alphabetically allows me to learn their names more quickly and it sets the tone I want.

My new freshman will push boundaries at some point, and this happens every year. They will become so unruly that teaching the way I want to (groups, PowerPoints, discussions, etc.) will not be possible. At that point, I inform them that they will be silently reading documents and writing short essays individually every day until I feel they are ready for something a bit more mature. I won't be "teaching" while this goes on. This usually takes 4-7 days and a lot of photocopying. It is also some work to find materials that keep them on topic and on pace with the course. During this time, I have had students threaten to go to Guidance, my Department Chair, or the Assistant Principal to complain. I then inform them that complaints that their teacher is making them read and analyze documents and write about those documents usually don't go very far, but they are welcome to try. At some point, a class leader or two will emerge and beg that I go back to "teaching". I do this, but I keep more individual essay work on my desk where students can see it. Sometimes I reach for it. Usually, I don't have to go back to it. At that point, I have the class where I need them to be.

5. *Friday Assessment Day!* Every Friday I give my students some kind of assessment. Some weeks it is just ten multiple choice questions. Other weeks, they may have to analyze a few documents and write a paragraph. Once a month I give a full test. Regardless of the topic

or format, my students know they will be assessed every Friday. It gives them a chance to show me what they know and a chance to make up for any low grades they may have gotten previously. I know that many teachers will say that they don't have the time to lose one day a week. You may be right. In that case I give a very short assessment followed by a reading that continues my curriculum. Slower students can take the reading home while faster ones will finish by the end of the period. To be honest, I look forward to assessment Fridays as well. I get to see how the students handle different types of assessments and it is a break from teaching like a maniac all week. Plus, in a data driven world, I have more numbers than I know what to do with.

If you are reading this, it means you care about your teaching. Many of the aforementioned methods may seem simple or elementary to you. Some might call them 'no brainers' and that's because they are already using many of them. The keys to owning the classroom are simple. Love your subject and be a student of it, find great materials, control the classroom (it's yours), and give the students many chances to show what they know.

Christopher Ferraro is a teacher at Spring Valley High School in Rockland County, NY. He holds Masters Degrees in Social Studies Education and European History from the City University of New York and recently received his Doctorate in Modern World History from St. John's University.

NOTES

CHAPTER 11

YOU!!!

(The MOST Important factor)

● ● ●

No quote is needed here. **You are the most important piece in the puzzle.** Over 50% of inner city teachers quit before they have completed five years of service. An inner city teacher ranks in the top three of the most stressful careers. Teachers in the suburbs have an enormous amount of stress as well. Just consider:

1. Dealing with the students
2. Rising to the expectations of the district
3. Answering to the parents and standardized test scores
4. Working for hours on lesson plans
5. Going to graduate school to earn more credits so you can master your craft

These are just some of the multitude of things that are part of a teaching career. You probably won't get rich from teaching; however, there is money to be made in curriculum writing, tutoring, publishing articles and more. My guess is that if you were solely motivated by money, you wouldn't be reading this guidebook in the first place.

You must take care of yourself both physically and emotionally. You should always be reading a pleasure book. As Emily Dickinson writes, "There is no frigate like a book, to take us lands away." If your life is all about your work, then forgive me for saying this, but you don't have much of a life. You deserve a life outside of the classroom. See movies, travel, and learn how to relieve stress.

An Exercise for You

Proper breathing is the best way to relieve stress. Close your eyes and inhale slowly and deeply. Now exhale slowly and fully until you can't expend any more air. Repeat this process slowly two to four times. Then breathe normally for two minutes or so. Focus on the number one and concentrate deeply. If the number starts disappearing, focus on the number two. You will feel very relaxed when this is over. If you feel dizzy during any part of this exercise, stop! Be sure you are not breathing in and out too quickly during the first part of this relaxation technique.

Always learn. Read books about your profession. Attend workshops of YOUR choice and always know that you can be a better teacher no matter how many years you have spent in the classroom. You are a special human being because you have dedicated your life to helping children. I know you will feel as successful and fulfilled as I still do after 33 years. I look forward to the next 33 years whether I am in or out of the classroom. Thank you for giving me the opportunity to share my thoughts and beliefs with you. Good luck in your career and remember... **Positive Reinforcement is the Key!**

Contact Marc Hoberman at info@gradesuccess.com
Visit us at www.marchoberman.com or www.gradesuccess.com

Marc Hoberman is available for presentations, consulting, and Staff Development.

You can also email Marc at marc@marchoberman.com

NOTES

Date: **Class:**   **Period:**   **Teacher:**

Learning Target:

DO NOW:

MOTIVATION:

DEVELOPMENT:

KEY TERMS:

SUMMARY:

HOMEWORK:

Letter home. This can be adjusted for emails as well.

(School letterhead here)

To the parent of _____
Please note that your son/daughter is having trouble in the following areas.

____ homework   ____ preparation
____ classwork   ____ self control
____ behavior   ____ testing
____ language   ____ other

I am certain that if we work together, we can help _____
to improve his/her difficulties. Please feel free to contact me at
_____ (insert SCHOOL phone number, SCHOOL email
address, DEPARTMENT phone #, etc). If you would like to schedule a
meeting, please let me know at your earliest convenience. Please sign this
letter and have your child return it to me tomorrow.

Respectfully,

_____   _____
Teacher Signature   Chairperson Signature
Subject

_____
Parent Signature

Have your chairperson or AP sign the original and then you can make
copies. You might want to make copies of all letters you send home to keep
for your records. Having your chairperson sign is usually a good idea so he
or she can troubleshoot any problems before they arise.

INSERT YOUR CLASS HEADING HERE
(Possible Contract for students and parents).

1. No foul language
2. No hats (Bad hair days are your problem, not mine.)
3. Raise your hand to ask or answer a question
4. Never throw your work out
5. Garbage gets thrown out at the end of the period (I hate when they get up and throw garbage away when I am teaching. It distracts me and is rude.)
6. You are responsible for all work even if you are absent
7. The period is over when I say so, the bell means nothing to me. (I do not allow kids to pack up before I dismiss class. Those who do are made to leave last.)
8. Bring a Loose-leaf Notebook, two pens and two pencils EVERY day. (I don't lend pens, I rent supplies. They cost points or a phone call home. I used to take money but not anymore.)

I have them sign the contract and the parent signs as well. I then make copies of the contract and keep one set and return the others to the students. They have to keep it in their notebooks. I like to have an outline in front of me indicating the rules I would like to be in my contract. However, I allow the students to create some of the rules that will be part of the contract for several reasons:

A. Their rules are usually more stringent than mine.
B. They take class very seriously when they have taken part in the creation of the contract.
C. This allows them to have OWNERSHIP of some of the management of the classroom.

ADD YOUR GRADING POLICY HERE AS WELL AS TWO
SPACES FOR STUDENT AND PARENT SIGNATURE.

_____   _____
Student Signature   Parent Signature

Letter home for movies that might be somewhat controversial.

School Letterhead

Date:

Dear Parents or Guardians:

Your child is currently involved in studying_____

_____

(describe unit of study and class, if appropriate). It is our intention to use the videotape_____(title) on _____(date) because _____

_____

(describe the use of this videotape in relation to your academic goals and objectives).

This letter is being sent to you in compliance with the District policy requiring parents/guardians to approve the intended use of videotapes or films which are not owned, broadcast, or recommended by the District prior to their scheduled showing. As part of that policy, we ask you to complete the form below, authorizing or exempting your child from the videotape showing. Please return your completed form to your child's teacher. Students exempted from this showing will be required to complete an alternative assignment. Should you have any questions regarding the videotape, please contact me.

_____

Signature of principal

(From <u>Using Film in the High School Curriculum: A Practical Guide For Teachers and Librarians</u> by Kenneth E. Resch and Vicki D. Schicker)

Sample Form

_____ *School District*

_____School

Statement Regarding Videotape or Film Use

(For Material Which Is Not Owned, Broadcast, or Recommended by the District)

Date: _____

Teacher's Name_____ Room_____

Title or description of
program:

_____

Producer (if known): _____

Network (if known): _____

        Material: Rented   _____

        Purchased   _____

        Taped at home   _____

Parental permission required: Yes _____ No_____

I plan to use the above program in my classroom on _____ (date) for the following reason (describe its use in relation to your academic goals and objectives:

_____

This program complies with the school's policy on the evaluation and selection of instructional materials. It is appropriate for the grade level and the instructional content enhances the curriculum. If this program has been recorded off-air, I affirm that it will be erased according to "fair use" interpretations of federal copyright regulations.

_____

Teacher's signature

Approved: _____   _____

        Principal's signature   Date

WEBSITES FOR LESSON PLANS

(These change often)

http://teachers.net/lessons/
http://www.edhelper.com/
http://www.teachnet.com/
http://www.teachnet.com/lesson/
http://www.education-world.com/a_tsl/
http://www.lessonplanspage.com/
http://www.lessonplanspage.com/
http://lessonplanz.com/
http://education.indiana.edu/cas/ttforum/lesson.html
http://www.atozteacherstuff.com/
http://www.askeric.org/Virtual/Lessons/
http://www.pbs.org/teachersource/
http://www.teachersfirst.com/
http://www.csun.edu/~hcedu013/plans.html
http://www.theteacherscorner.net/
http://www.col-ed.org/cur/

ABOUT THE AUTHOR

• • •

Keynote Speaker, Seminar Leader, Consultant, and author, Marc Hoberman is the Director and Lead Facilitator of Grade Success, Inc. He has trained students, teachers, and corporate executives nationally through a variety of Personal Improvement and Training Methods. Marc has been featured on both television and radio. He has also led workshops at the New Jersey and New York State Reading Conferences as well as the International YAI Conference. Marc has presented seminars at the Tristate Camping conference for 7 years in a row and is the Staff Writer for Canada Camps Magazine. He was a featured speaker at the New England Camping Conference and the Canada Camping Conference as well. As a freelance writer for NY Parents Metro Magazine, Marc has shared his wealth of educational expertise with thousands of parents each year. From the classroom to the boardroom, Marc continues his mission to "help people realize their full potential."

Marc is also the author of the memoir Search and Seizure: Overcoming Illness and Adversity which is available on Amazon.com and Kindle and multiple ebook formats. The memoir tells his story of being diagnosed with epilepsy as a teenager, an illness he kept secret for over 34 years. Marc makes presentations about overcoming adversity at high schools, colleges and parent groups.

Marc lives in Rockland County, New York with his wife Ivy, sons Craig and Scott and his Havanese daughter, Maggie.

Made in the USA
Columbia, SC
08 September 2021

45076419R00048